Growing up
BETWEEN THE WARS

Frances Wilkins

B.T. Batsford Ltd *London* A7.50

ISBN 0 7134 0775 1

Printed and bound in Great Britain by
Anchor Brendon Ltd,
Tiptree, Essex
for the Publishers Batsford Academic and
Educational, an imprint of
B T Batsford Limited
4 Fitzhardinge Street, London W1H 0AH

Acknowledgment

The Author and Publishers would like to thank the
following for their kind permission to reproduce
copyright illustrations:
    J.S. Gray for figs 7 and 23; GLC Photographic
Unit Department of Architecture and Civic Design
for figs 5, 35, 36, 37 and 38; The Librarian, East
Sussex County Libraries for fig 40; London
Transport Executive for figs 1, 24, and 42; Leigh
Public Library for fig 21; Radio Times Hulton
Picture Library for figs 2, 4, 6, 8, 10, 11, 14, 15, 16,
17, 18, 19, 20, 25, 26, 27, 29, 30, 31, 32, 33, 34,
39, 41, 43, 44, 45, 46, 47, 48, 49, 50, 51, 52, 53;
J. Sainsbury Ltd for fig 22; Wates Ltd for fig 3;
Josiah Wedgwood & Sons Ltd for fig 9; and Miss D.
Wilcockson for fig 28.

Contents

The Illustrations

1 Between the Wars

Post-war hopes

The First World War ended in November, 1918. It had lasted over four years and had cost more than a million young British lives. The politicians had promised, however, that once the War was over Britain would become "a land fit for heroes to live in", and so people were looking forward to a period of peace and prosperity.

The economy

For a year or two all appeared to be going well. Industry of all kinds began to expand, and both wages and profits were high. But

1 A variety of vehicles (motorcars, open-topped and closed buses, motorbikes and side-cars, a bicycle and an ice-cream cart) at Burford Bridge, Boxhill, 1924

by 1921 it was clear that the country was facing an economic depression. Cheap foreign goods were pouring onto the British market, while British products were becoming too expensive to find buyers abroad.

Both the employers and the government blamed the workers for this state of affairs. They said that the workers' wages were too high, and that this was forcing up the price of British goods. The employers tried to persuade the trade unions to accept wage cuts for the workers, but they refused, and the majority of employers then had no alternative but to reduce the size of their work-force.

Many employers were installing more modern machinery in their factories, and this also almost invariably meant that they required fewer workers to produce the same amount of goods. As a result, by the 1930s there were nearly three million men out of work, and another three or four million who worked only part-time.

Unemployment

The unemployment was not general all over the country, however. It was confined chiefly to what were called the "old industries", like coal, cotton, shipbuilding and steel. In some

2   A one-man unemployment demonstration in the 1930s

3   The entrance to one of Wates the builders' estates of new houses

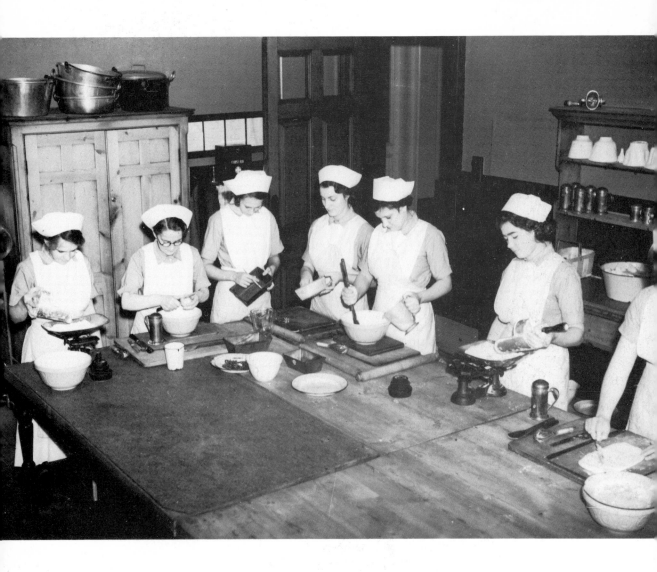

mining villages in Wales and Scotland, for example, practically all the men were out of work, and in the shipbuilding areas of North-East England two out of three men were on the dole. On the other hand, the so-called "new industries" were still expanding. These were, for instance, the car, aircraft, rayon and chemical industries, which relied on a high degree of technology. Most of these industries were situated in the Midlands or the South of England, and in these regions unemployment was always comparatively low.

The government did little to help the "depressed areas", as the areas of unemployment were called. It seemed overwhelmed by the size of the problem. Even when the first Labour Government was formed, in 1924, Britain still continued to become more and more sharply divided between the "haves" and the "have-nots". Indeed, the very conditions, like the import of cheap foreign goods and the installation of new machinery in the factories, which were the cause of the unemployment, benefited the people who were lucky enough to have jobs. For the

8

result was that the price of almost everything was brought down and all kinds of things, which would have been considered luxuries before the War, became available to vast numbers of ordinary people.

Housing
Housing was one of the first areas to reap the reward of lower prices. Labour was cheap and easy to find, because of the unemployment, and building materials were also very cheap. In the 1919 Housing Act the government promised to give the local councils a subsidy for every house they built, and in the interwar years around 1.5 million council houses were erected. During the same period 2.5 million houses were also put up by private builders. Many of them could be bought on a mortgage for as little as 8/10d (44p) per week. Neither the council nor the private houses were within the means of the unemployed, however, who mostly continued to live in cramped, insanitary slums.

4 Girls training to be maids at Lapswood Domestic Training Centre, Sydenham, September 1938

During the 1920s most better-off people still employed maids. But as time went on, girls would only "go into service" if they could not find a job in a factory or a shop. There were still plenty of "chars", however, who would clean for about 6d (2½p) per hour. In any case, the compact modern houses were very easy to run.

Entertainment
New forms of entertainment were cheap too, for people who could afford them at all. In 1922, for example, the first radio play was heard on the air. This was the beginning of regular BBC broadcasts, and within a few years almost every house in the more prosperous parts of the country had a "wireless" aerial on its roof. People could also go to the cinema for as little as 9d (3½p) a seat. In the early post-war years films were still silent, and accompanied by music on huge cinema organs. In 1928 the first "talkies" reached the British screens, however, and cinema-going became even more popular than before.

5 The oriental-style Palace Cinema, Southall, advertising an "All talking" film

6   The original, 7-horse-power "Baby Austin",
which appeared in 1922. It cost £165, seated 4, and
could go at 40 miles (64 kilometres) per hour. It
went out of production in 1938

Motoring
Cheap motoring also became available in the
late 1920s. In fact, it was soon possible to
buy a brand new Ford car for as little as £99.
This altered the whole pattern of living for
many people, and meant that for the first
time they could go for outings to the seaside
or visit relations at the weekends.

Holidays
Holidays became more commonplace during
this period. In 1937 the first Butlin holiday
camp was opened, where working people
could enjoy themselves at a reasonable cost.
The following year the government passed
an act which encouraged employers (although

it did not compel them) to give their work-people one week's paid holiday every year.

Families

Another important factor in the improved standard of living for many people was the reduced size of families. One or two children became the accepted average, instead of the five or six common before the First World War. Ironically, however, it was mainly the people in work who restricted the size of their families, while the unemployed often continued to have as many children as before.

Many people who were children between the Wars must have happy memories. If their fathers were in work, life was comfortable, and it appeared to be getting better every day. But for countless others in the "depressed areas" whose fathers were on the dole, the outbreak of the Second World War in August, 1939 must have come as an almost welcome change.

2 Homes

New building

There was a desperate shortage of houses immediately after the First World War. Soldiers returning from the Front found it impossible even to rent a few rooms for their families. The result was that new houses were soon springing up everywhere, either for people to buy with the help of a building society, or else for them to rent from the local council.

Unfortunately, these new houses were often built along the sides of main roads. This meant that the appearance of the countryside was spoilt for mile after mile by unplanned "ribbon development". It also meant that the houses were too spread out for most of the inhabitants to have any real community life, which was a particular shame for the children.

Some of the new "ribbon development" was made up of neat bungalows. Before the First World War bungalows had been almost unknown, but they became very popular, afterwards, with the slightly better-off. They cost more than houses because they occupied

7   Houses being built along the side of what had been a narrow road, in Patcham, 1932. An example of "ribbon development" beginning

8   A typical sitting-room of between the Wars

more ground space, but they had the great advantage, from the housewife's point of view, that they had no tiring stairs either to climb or to clean.

The homes built between the Wars were not usually very attractive. Indeed, nearly all the houses in the new "ribbon development" were nothing but dull little boxes. In the 1920s they generally had pebble-dash outside walls and slate roofs, but by the '30s they were mostly built of red brick and had roofs of red tiles. Among the well-to-do, "mock Tudor" homes were very fashionable, and some of the better-off thought it was smart to live in curious cube-shaped houses

with flat roofs. Whatever their appearance, however, most homes built between the Wars had one great asset: they nearly all had their own garden where the children could play and enjoy the fresh air.

The standard of house-building varied considerably between the Wars. Some of the new houses were solidly constructed, but others were only shoddily built — "jerry-built", as people described them. There was no government control over the building industry, and if people found, when they moved in, that their house was "jerry-built", there was no one to whom they could turn for redress.

Apart from the homes of the well-to-do, all the houses were built to much the same pattern. Upstairs there were three bedrooms, a toilet and (except in a few of the worst new council houses) a bathroom. Downstairs there was a lounge, a dining-room and a kitchen. Some of the privately built houses had garages, but these were almost unknown in the council-built properties.

Interiors

The interiors of the new houses were almost as dull as the outsides. The walls were usually distempered (rather than papered) in a neutral shade, such as cream or pale green. Pictures were unfashionable and were rarely seen in smart homes, although there was generally a picture-rail to break the monotony of the completely bare walls.

Even the furniture between the Wars was designed to be plain and functional. In fact, the height of fashion in the '20s was for chromium-plated, tubular furniture. By the '30s people had realized that this was as uncomfortable as it looked, however, and the new craze was to have all the furniture as cube-like as possible. The fashionable colours were black, white and orange, and the floral patterns of earlier times had been almost completely superseded by geometrical designs. There was no plastic, but in the '30s there was "bakelite", which was often used for making such things as the casings for radios, although it cracked rather easily.

Central heating was unknown in private homes between the Wars. People usually had an open fire in their lounge, surrounded by a tiled fireplace, a tiled hearth and a built-in, tiled fender. There was generally an open fire in the kitchen as well, with a boiler behind it, and this provided all the hot water for the house, both downstairs and upstairs.

There was no wall-to-wall carpeting in ordinary people's homes at this period. Better-off families had large square or oblong carpets, surrounded by polished parquet flooring. Most working-class people had to be content with linoleum, however, and a few small rugs which they placed in front of their fires or beside their beds.

Electricity

One of the greatest advantages of the new houses was that they were all lit by electricity. This not only gave a bright, clear light but

9   A Wedgwood coronation mug which must have been found in many homes between the Wars. It was designed originally as a souvenir of the coronation of Edward VIII. This never took place, however, since Edward abdicated. The same design was used for the souvenir coronation mugs of George VI and Elizabeth II

10   This "Super Het" washing machine, designed by Mrs Peace of Sheffield, gained a silver medal at an Inventions Exhibition held in 1937. The machine was entirely rust-proof. To make it work, you pulled the handle to and fro. The sides acted as scrubbing boards inside. The piece of wood attached is the ironing board

14

also came on at the touch of a switch. Most of the older houses at this period were still lit by gas, or, in the case of houses and cottages in the country, by oil-lamps and candles.

With the introduction of electricity came various new domestic appliances. Electric irons, toasters and vacuum cleaners, for example, had all become fairly commonplace by the '30s. There was, indeed, an ever-increasing demand for these new labour-saving gadgets, as more and more middle-class housewives stopped employing maids and had to run their homes themselves.

There were no modern washing-machines between the Wars, however. Some house-wives had a "copper", as it was called, but this only boiled the clothes and did not rinse or spin-dry them. Most working-class women used a scrubbing-board and a large iron mangle, while the better-off usually sent all their dirty linen to a laundry. People did not have refrigerators in their homes at this period, either. But many families had an "ice-box", which was a metal-lined chest in which they placed blocks of ice. This kept butter and milk cool, but it was not cold enough to keep ice-cream frozen. The housewives usually bought the blocks of ice from the local fishmonger.

Not all families lived in new houses be-tween the Wars, of course. In fact, in 1939 two-thirds of the population still lived in houses built in Edwardian and Victorian times. But the new fashions in furniture, decoration and the general way of life affected most families, and provided the background against which most of the children of that period grew up.

3 Clothes

Women's clothing

Before the First World War women still wore ankle-length clothes. Everyone knew, of course, that women and girls must have legs, but it was considered immodest to show them. Then, shortly after the War, a revolutionary change took place. Women began wearing dresses that barely reached to their calves, and were sometimes even shorter. What was more, these dresses were no longer elaborate, restrictive garments. Instead, they were as plain and shapeless as it was possible to make them. In fact, the height of fashion was a dress that looked just like a straight tube, with no tucks or gathers of any kind, and (in the summer) without any sleeves.

Girls' clothing

Little girls naturally benefited from the new fashions as well. For the first time for centuries they were able to run about and play, unhindered by any heavy, cumbersome clothes. In the summer, for example, they wore simple, sleeveless shifts which ended well above the knee, no stockings or socks, and only light canvas shoes.

Even in the winter their clothes were simple by earlier standards. A plain serge skirt and a hand-knitted jumper were the commonest form of dress. Coats were also plain, although they often had fur collars and cuffs, and no well brought-up little girl ever went out without a hat and a pair of gloves.

Girls no longer had to wear layers of petticoats, either. But on cold days they wore winceyette "liberty bodices", with suspenders to keep up their woollen stockings. Small girls also wore gaiters, if their parents could afford them. These were usually made of soft leather, done up with a dozen or more shoe-buttons, and they stretched from the foot to well above the knee.

Throughout the whole of the '20s and '30s girls' clothes remained simple. But the dresses gradually became more shapely and had a more pronounced waist. By the late '30s one of the most popular styles had a full-length skirt, a wide sash round the waist tied in a bow at the back, puffed sleeves and a dainty lace-edged collar.

Hairstyles

With the new styles of clothes for girls came new hairstyles. Before the First World War practically every little girl grew her hair long and had it tied up with ribbons. After the War, however, many girls had their hair cut short in a "bob", as it was called, or even "shingled", which meant that it was cut almost as short as a boy's at the back. Girls with "bobbed" hair often put it in wet rags at night in order to curl it. The better-off sometimes had a "marcel wave" at the hairdresser's, which meant that the hair was waved with hot tongs. The girls who still had long hair usually wore it in two plaits ("pigtails", as they were called), with a bow at the end of each, at least when they went to school.

Men's clothing

Men's clothes showed almost as marked a

Underwear Styles for Growing Girls

No. 9826 No. 9827. No. 9828. No. 9829. No. 9828.

A CHILD'S BODICE AND
KNICKERS.
No. 9826.
In sizes for 4 and 6 years.

A GIRL'S BODICE AND
KNICKERS.
No. 9827.
In sizes for 8 and 10 years.

A SQUARE-NECKED
COMBINATION.
No. 9828.
In sizes for 10 and 12 years.

A ROUND-NECKED COMBINA-
TION WITH FLAP CLOSING.
No. 9829.
In sizes for 6 and 8 years.

The figure in the top right-hand corner shows
a second way of trimming Pattern No. 9828.

Paper Patterns, price 5½d. each, postage
1d. each extra by unsealed packet post,
or 1½d. by letter post. Address to the
"Girl's Own" Fashion Editor, 4, Bouverie
Street, Fleet Street, London, E.C. 4.

Showing another way
of making up Pattern
No. 9826

A JUMPER STYLE SLEEPING-
SUIT.
No. 9830.
In sizes for 8 and 10 years.

11 Ladies' fashion, 1920s

12 An underwear advertisement from *The Girls' Own Paper*, 1928

13 Fashionable wide trousers worn by Matt Busby, Liverpool F.C. and Scottish International, in 1937, as he coaches Len Langford of Mosley Road School, Manchester. Len's father, Sam Langford, famous Manchester United goalkeeper, watches, in a pair of "plus-fours" — also fashionable

change as the women's at this period. Before the War every middle-class man was expected to wear a dark suit with a waistcoat, whatever the weather. After the War, however, grey flannel trousers and a tweed jacket, or even a sleeveless pullover in the summer, became

accepted as everyday wear. Men also wanted to have more choice in the way they dressed, and so styles like "plus-fours", the baggy knickerbockers originally intended to be worn on the golf course, became popular. So, from 1924 onwards, did "Oxford bags". These were wide, flapping, flannel trousers, sometimes 60 centimetres or more around their deep turn-ups.

Boys' clothing
Younger boys were allowed to show their knees for the first time in the early '20s. Gone were the thick tweed knickerbockers and heavy woollen socks of the pre-war years. Most boys by this time were dressed in short

14   Boys and girls in the playground of Stan Road School, Fulham, 1935. Their clothes are "between-the-Wars": sleeveless shifts, no stockings, light shoes, above-the-knee trousers, etc

trousers, a long-sleeved, woollen jumper with a small collar but no tie, and knee-length, turned-down, woollen socks. Slightly older boys often wore shirts and sleeveless Fair Isle pullovers instead of jumpers. These pull-overs were mass-produced in bright reds, greens and blues, in traditional Fair Isle patterns. They not only looked cheerful but also hid the braces which all boys wore at that period, because their trousers did not fit snugly enough round the waist to stay up by themselves.

21

Poor boys still wore heavy boots that laced up round their ankles. These were cumbersome and uncomfortable, but their parents thought that they lasted well. Better-off boys, however, always wore shoes or, in the summer, the same type of light canvas sandals as their sisters.

Uniforms

Children who went to the free elementary schools (see the next chapter) hardly ever wore a school uniform. It was all most poor families could do to afford even one set of clothes for their children. In fact, "No boots to wear" was one of the commonest excuses for children not attending school in some of the poorer parts of the country.

On the other hand, children at fee-paying schools almost invariably wore a uniform. For girls, this was normally a pleated gymslip, a blouse, a school tie and black or brown woollen stockings. Over this they wore a cardigan, and, in the cold weather, a serge coat. They also wore felt hats in the winter and panamas in the summer, both with a ribbon in the school colours. Boys at fee-paying schools usually wore a grey serge suit with either short or long trousers. They wore a tie in the school colours, and a striped cap to match. Blazers were worn generally in the summer only, with white trousers and open-necked shirts, for cricket or on other informal occasions.

Materials

Most clothes between the Wars were made out of natural fibres. This meant, in the main, wool and cotton and sometimes, for better-off people, linen and silk. There were only two man-made materials — rayon and artificial silk — and both were worn mainly by the poorer people, as they were cheap and regarded generally as being rather shoddy.

4 Education

Free elementary schools

Between the Wars 95% of the nation's children began their school life, as soon as they had had their fifth birthday, in a free elementary school. Most of these schools belonged to the state, but some were voluntary schools. This usually meant that they belonged either to the Church of England or to the Roman Catholic Church.

15   Children at an open-air school in St James's Park, 1927. The purpose of open-air schools was to keep children who were brought up in smokey towns and cities, where lung conditions were common, out in a reasonably pollution-free atmosphere for as long as possible

In the majority of schools conditions were by no means ideal. The buildings were usually old (especially in the case of the church schools), and they often looked more like prisons than schools. They were ill-lit, badly ventilated and often had only the most primitive sanitary arrangements. There were no gyms, no playing fields and no facilities at all for practical work. There was also appalling overcrowding in many schools. The government's aim was that classes should be of 50 or less, but classes of 60 or even more were not uncommon. For this reason teaching was extremely formal, and almost the entire day was spent on the three R's, except for brief periods of drill (a regimented type of P.E.).

16   A Lacrosse match between schoolgirls from the North and South of England, April 1923

During the 1930s quite a number of new schools were built. These were usually airy and bright, and had large glass doors leading onto pleasant playgrounds and lawns. Unfortunately, even by 1939 only 25% of the elementary schools were like this, and they were almost exclusively in the better-off small towns and suburbs.

All elementary schools were open at least 48 weeks a year. The average working-class family was not expected to have the money to take its children away for long holidays. On the other hand, schools were open only during the actual teaching hours. There were usually no school dinners, and little or nothing in the way of out-of-class activities, such as football, music or school clubs.

Well over 90% of the children between the Wars stayed at the same free elementary school until they were 14. Then their education was considered to be complete, and they had to find themselves a job. This was usually fairly easy, despite the high level of unemployment, as firms were always glad to take on school-leavers for a year or two at very low rates of pay, and then dismiss them as soon as they demanded adult wages.

17   A Geography lesson at the Licensed Victuallers' School, Slough, in 1935

Fee-paying schools

As well as the free elementary schools, there were various types of fee-paying private schools. Rich parents sent their children to kindergartens and preparatory schools, and then to public schools when the children reached the age of 13. Most middle-class people, however, had to be content with small private schools for their children up to the age of 11, and then they sent them as fee-paying pupils to a secondary school.

The standard in the small private schools varied considerably. Some were well-run and progressive, while others were little more than child-minding establishments. Anyone could open a school, and a certain number

of unscrupulous people did so, taking advantage of the horror that many middle-class parents felt at the thought of sending their children to the free elementary schools. Even in the well-run private schools the teachers were often unqualified. They had learnt whatever they knew about teaching by spending a year or two as "pupil-teachers", helping more experienced teachers. Also, the premises used as private schools had rarely been designed as schools. They were usually just private houses, with small, odd-shaped rooms, and little or nothing in the way of a playground.

Nevertheless, the advantages of the private schools were obvious. The classes were small and had none of the lice-ridden, unwashed urchins who were often found in the state schools. Also, the parents knew something of the way in which their children were being educated, as they rarely did in the state schools, with their large notices "No parents admitted" on the gates.

Secondary schools

A certain proportion of "scholarship" children were accepted by the private fee-paying secondary schools. Children at a free elementary school could sit an examination at the age of 11 to try to win a scholarship to a private secondary school. Winning a scholarship meant that the child had a free place at the secondary school, or, after 1932, that the parents paid for the child to go there according to their means. Only 7% of free elementary school children did go on to secondary education, as there was naturally considerable competition to get into one of these secondary shcools. Also, in the main, it was only children from slightly better-off homes whose parents let them sit the entrance examination. The really poor either wanted their children to leave school and go to work as soon as possible, or else they could not afford the uniform and various other items required by the secondary schools.

In most of the secondary schools the syllabus was extremely narrow. Nearly all the children learnt French, but very few of them had the opportunity to learn a second modern language. Three times as many children studied Latin as Physics, and subjects such as Social Studies and Economics were virtually unknown.

The government was well aware that the free-school system was unsatisfactory. In particular, it was felt that children over the age of 11 should not remain in the same schools as the younger ones. And so, in the late '20s, a number of senior schools were opened for the children who did not win "scholarships". However, in 1931 government economy measures put an end to this reorganization.

Higher education

Very few children between the Wars could expect to go on to higher education. The universities, for example, were reserved largely for pupils from public schools whose parents were able to pay. On average, fewer than 5% of the children leaving the secondary schools went on to university, and only about the same number of secondary school children were accepted for teachers' training colleges.

It was particularly difficult for girls to receive higher education. And if they did so, they could usually only expect to follow their professional careers until they were married. Very few county councils, for instance, would employ married women teachers, and nearly all the branches of the Civil Service dismissed a woman the moment they learnt she was married.

Vocational training

Free vocational training hardly existed between the Wars. If a girl wished to learn typing, for example, she normally had to go to a commercial college, for which her parents had to pay. Most school-leavers who

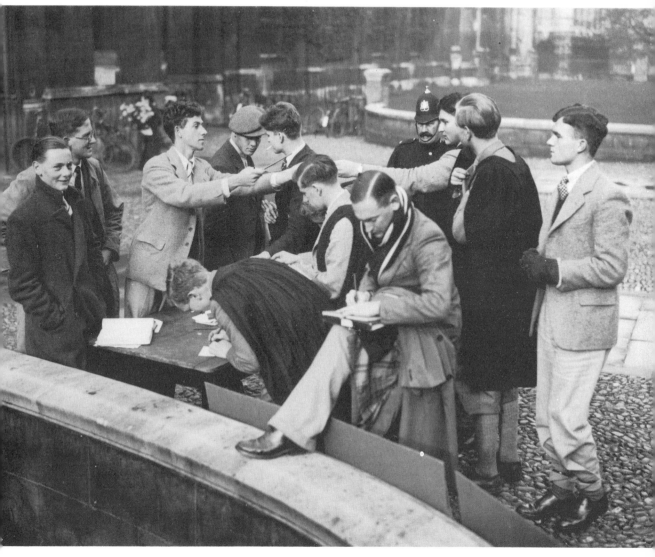

wished to learn a skill became apprentices, however, and then put aside some of their wages so that they could afford to attend an evening institute.

18 Cambridge undergraduates outside King's College in November 1935. They were holding a mock election at the same time as the national poll was taking place

5 Entertainment

The cinema
Easily the most popular form of entertainment between the Wars was the cinema.

19 Rudolph Valentino was a favourite film star. Here members of the Valentino International Memorial Society commemorate the anniversary of his death by decorating a photograph of him

Even the most impoverished parts of the country had their glittering new "picture palaces" (picture 5), as they were generally called. It has been estimated that among city-dwellers about 40% of the people went to the pictures at least once a week, and approximately 25% went twice or even three times a week.

20 A hand-wound gramophone

In the early 1920s the films were still silent. The words the actors were saying had to be flashed on to the screen in the form of short captions. There was always some kind of appropriate musical accompaniment, however, usually provided in the bigger cinemas by enormous electric cinema organs.

From about 1928 onwards the cinemas began to show "talkies". These were nearly all made in Hollywood and had an immediate and startling effect on the way in which people in our country spoke. Children, in particular, were soon saying "OK", "sez you" and "no kidding", and talking about people being "bumped off" and criminals being arrested by the "cops".

The first popular cartoon character, Felix the Cat, made his appearance in 1923. Mickey Mouse arrived six years later, and was quickly followed by numerous other amusing cartoon creations. There were no full-length cartoon films, though, until 1938, when Walt Disney produced his famous *Snow-White*, which was an instant success with children all over the world.

Saturday morning shows for children were popular by the early '30s. They consisted chiefly of Westerns, and a few short cartoon films generally featuring Mickey Mouse or Donald Duck. Children needed only a few coppers to enjoy themselves for a whole morning, and for another penny or two they could even have one of the latest treats of the period — a "choc-ice" - in the interval.

Gramophones
At home, people liked to listen to the gramophone. This was like a record-player, but it was clockwork and had to be wound up by hand. All the records turned at 78 r.p.m., and played for a few minutes only. They were also extremely brittle, and always had to be handled with the greatest possible care.

The wireless
An increasing number of people also had a "wireless" or radio. In the '20s the wireless was still in its infancy, and only a few enthusiasts "listened in" with the aid of a pair of head-phones. But by the '30s practically

every middle-class family had a wireless aerial on the roof, and there were round-the-clock broadcasts from several different stations. By the '30s there was even a regular "Children's Hour" on the wireless. This was a programme of stories, plays and other short features introduced by a radio "uncle" and "aunt". The wireless also gave many children their first opportunity to hear really good music, especially after the famous BBC Symphony Orchestra was founded in 1930.

21 People formed wireless discussion groups like this one, meeting to listen to and discuss programmes at Leigh Public Library, 1930

22 These are Sainsbury's employees in fancy dress. To promote sales they processed with decorated tricycles or vans through the town. To advertise Blue Kaddy tea these people have used the theme of Amy Johnson, who was making headlines in the early 1930s with her long-distance solo aeroplane flights

Music

Many children, of course, liked playing an instrument themselves and, if they went to a secondary school, they sometimes had the opportunity to play in a school orchestra. There were no recorders, though, except in museums, as no one had realized that these lovely old instruments could be used to help children to read and appreciate music.

31

Dancing

Dancing was immensely popular at this period. Nearly all middle-class little girls (and some small boys) went to dancing classes even before they went to school. They usually learnt ballet, tap or Greek dancing, and at the age of eleven or twelve they began ball-room dancing, which meant the waltz, the foxtrot and the tango.

When they were older, better-off boys and girls usually met at their friends' homes and danced to the gramophone, or later to one of the large, expensive, new instruments called a "radiogram". But working-class youngsters generally went to a public dance hall or "palais de danse", as it was sometimes called, where they could dance to a band for several hours for a small admission fee. In the early '20s any kind of lively, exuberant dance was popular, providing it could be performed to one of the new jazz tunes that had just arrived from the States. In 1926, however, a crazy, boisterous dance called the Charleston arrived from America, and in a short time "doing the Charleston" became a mania all over the country.

Fancy dress

Another pleasant way for better-off people to spend an evening was to go to a fancy-dress party. These were extremely popular between the Wars both for adults and children. People particularly liked to dress up as historical characters, such as Napoleon or Queen Elizabeth I, and they usually either had their costumes made for them or hired them from theatrical costumiers.

Reading

Children in better-educated families naturally had plenty of books between the Wars, but the middle- and working-class children generally had far less opportunity to read than they have today. Public libraries did exist, but they rarely had children's sections, and in any case they were usually gloomy, forbidding-looking buildings with the word "Silence" written in large letters on every wall. In 1939 the position improved a little when the first "Penguin" paper-back books were published, costing only 6d (2½p) each. But most of the subjects appealed only to the better educated, and there were still no paper-backs of any kind published specifically with children in mind.

There were, on the other hand, a large number of children's magazines and comics. For the smallest children, for example, there were *Tiny Tots*, *Chick's Own* and *The Rainbow*. For older children there were comics like *The Magnet* (featuring Billy Bunter), and also the extremely well-produced and stimulating magazines called *The Boys' Own Paper* and *The Girls' Own Paper*.

There was also the famous *Children's Newspaper*. This was the idea of a well-known children's writer Arthur Mee, and it first appeared in 1919. The *Children's Newspaper* covered all the major events of the day in a simple, readable style, and tried to encourage children to take an intelligent interest in everything that was going on in the world.

6 Sports and Pastimes

It was between the Wars that spectator sports first began drawing enormous crowds. This was due partly to the fact that improved methods of transport made it much easier for people to reach the sports grounds and stadiums. But it was due also to the fact that shorter working hours (not to mention the high level of unemployment) gave people a great deal more leisure than they had ever had before.

Football

Football was by far the most popular spectator sport at this period. By the early 1920s well over half a million people were watching

23 Spectators at the football match between Brighton & Hove Albion and Corinthians, at Goldstone Ground, 13th January 1923. The result was a 1-1 draw. Attendance: 23,642. Receipts: £1,923

VIRGINIA WATER
BY MOTOR BUS

ROUTE 117A FROM
HOUNSLOW TOWN STATION

24 One of many London Transport posters announcing how to get to all popular destinations by public transport

professional football matches every Saturday afternoon in the season. The crowds naturally included countless youngsters, who were probably all dreaming of becoming professional footballers and playing for their favourite teams themselves when they grew up. There were no adequate facilities for most boys to practise football, however. Very few elementary schools had a playing field, and parks usually had a large notice saying "No ball games allowed". In fact, the majority of youngsters had nowhere to play but the streets, and their goal-posts were usually just a couple of rolled-up coats on the ground.

Summer sports
In the summer the most popular spectator sport was cricket. Indeed, far more people

25 Suzanne Lenglen at Wimbledon, July 1922

watched professional cricket between the Wars than either before that time or since. Once again, however, there were no proper places for boys to practise, and most of them had to chalk a wicket on a wall and play in the street.

Among the better-off one of the most popular sports was tennis. But poor children never took a great deal of interest in the game, because they could not afford the equipment. The really well-to-do had tennis courts laid out in their gardens, and held elegant tennis parties, while the middle-class youngsters usually hired a court for an hour in a local park.

New activities
There was also a new sport for better-off youngsters between the Wars. This was ice-skating. Before that time if people wanted to skate they had to wait for a pond or a lake to freeze over. But by the '20s it was possible to freeze water artificially by means of electricity, and fashionable new "skating-rinks" were soon to be found in every large city.

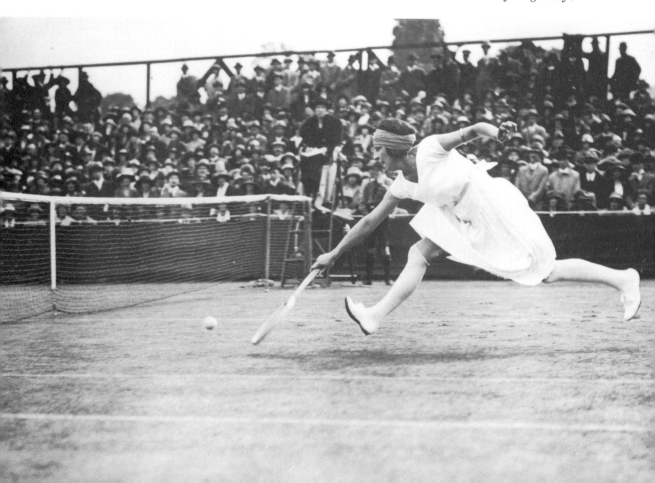

Swimming became increasingly popular between the Wars, as more and more families were able to afford regular visits to the seaside every year. But comparatively few children actually received lessons in swimming, as it was usually only the secondary schools that had swimming-pools or even took their pupils to the public baths for instruction. Sunbathing also became popular in the late '20s, even for girls. (Before the First World War people had always admired a girl with a pale, delicate complexion.) A great many youngsters began putting on a bathing-costume not just to swim, but to sit on the beach, or even in their back gardens, to try to get suntanned.

The word "hiking" was unknown until the early '30s. Then, almost overnight, young people discovered what fun it was to go for long walks in the country. "Hikers" were easy to recognize by their shorts and huge rucksacks, and also by the fact that they usually "hiked" in groups of any number from 4 or 5 to a hundred.

Cycling

Cycling was mainly a method of getting about in the '20s. In fact, it has been estimated that there were ten times as many cycles as cars on the road at that period. People did cycle for pleasure, though, and there were even occasional cycle races for young men who wanted to test their strength and endurance in this way. It was in the early '30s that cycling really became a popular sport, however. Cycling clubs were formed all over the country, and even special cyclists' cafés and guest houses were opened. The cyclists usually went in groups, and every weekend countless crowds of happy youngsters could be seen pedalling along on practically every main road.

If parents could afford it, they usually bought their small children a tricycle. These were larger than they are today, and children often rode them until they were eight or nine years old. Then, if they were lucky, their parents bought them a "fairy cycle", but they had to be able to ride properly, as stabilizers had not been invented at that time. Many children had to be content with a scooter, though. This was a two-wheeled affair, with a long base close to the ground, and a tall steering-rod at the front. The children held on to the steering-rod with their hands, put one foot on the base and "scooted" along with the other. Most poor children's scooters were home-made out of two lengths of rough wood.

Toys and games

Whips and tops were among the favourite toys of most children between the Wars. So were wooden hoops, which had to be guided along with the help of a short stick. Another new toy in the early '30s was the yo-yo. The moment it arrived in this country from America the yo-yo became a craze overnight.

Poorer children played all kinds of street games, like hopscotch and marbles. But it was a game with cigarette cards that was easily the favourite with the majority of children. A row of cards was leant up against the bottom of a wall, and the children took it in turns to try to knock the cards down by flicking other cigarette cards against them.

A new indoor pastime arrived from America in 1924. This was the crossword puzzle, and it was soon amusing and intriguing people everywhere. Originally, crosswords were designed for adults, but they soon began appearing in children's comics as well. Later on, such variations as "Lexicon" and "Scrabble" were invented.

Shortly after the first crosswords came "Monopoly". This was a tremendous craze, and in no time at all almost every better-off family had bought a "Monopoly" game for their children. By the standards of the time it was rather expensive, however, and most poorer families had to be content with such traditional games as "Snakes and Ladders" and "Ludo".

36

26 Hikers

7 Holidays

As soon as the First World War was over many wealthy people started going abroad for their holidays once again. If they had children they often went to Brittany, but Austria and Switzerland were very popular too. There was an excellent train service all over Europe and, in general, prices were far lower on the Continent than in England at that time.

For the rest of the population, of course, the position was different. Most ordinary working people had neither the money nor the time off from work to give much thought to holidays. An excursion to the sea on a Bank Holiday, or a few days with some

27   A family having a picnic lunch on the beach at Bognor, March 1921

relatives, was all that the average British family expected in the first few years after the War.

During the 1920s and '30s people's ideas gradually altered, however. They began to think that holidays were not merely fun, but also essential to health and well-being, especially in the case of young children. As a result, more and more families began to go away every year, until by 1939 more than 15 million people were enjoying an annual week's break from routine.

Means of transport

At first, the most popular place for a holiday was the seaside. There was a good rail service to most of the coastal resorts, and in the early '20s nearly everyone set off for their holidays in a train. The seaside traders were naturally quick to take advantage of the crowds of new visitors, and soon there were stalls selling buckets and spades, ice-cream, rock and candy floss on almost every seaside "prom".

The railways did not have it all their own way for very long, however. By the mid-'20s another means of transport, the charabanc, was carrying a large percentage of the holiday-makers every year. A charabanc was like a coach, with a canvas, fold-down roof, and it usually held twenty to thirty people, all sitting on transverse seats facing the driver. The charabanc had several advantages over the train. For one thing, it could go wherever the passengers wanted, and was not compelled to follow special tracks. For another, the charabanc ride itself was an exciting part of the holiday. With the roof folded down, the passengers could enjoy the fresh air and the sun, and see all the sights of the countryside.

But the greatest change of all in holiday habits was brought about by the car. By the '30s countless people, who would not have dreamed a few years before that they would

28 A charabanc, owned by Wilcockson Brothers of Middleton Junction, Lancashire

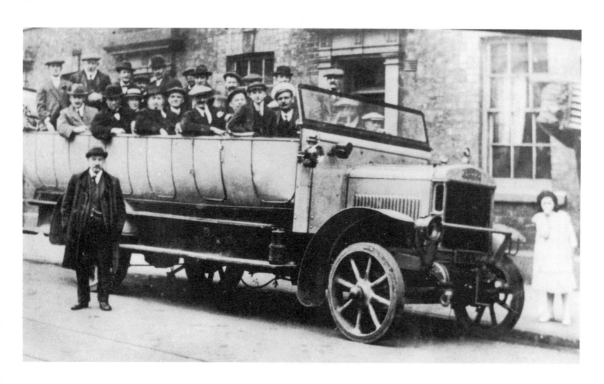

ever own a car, had become motorists. In fact, by 1939 there were more than one million private cars on the road, which meant that one family in ten had their own means of transport. There were also more than 600,000 motor-bikes. These were not generally regarded as a means of travelling at great speed, but were just the poor man's substitute for a car. Many of the motor-bikes had side-cars (picture 1), so that the motor-cyclist could take his wife and even one or two small children with him when he set off to enjoy himself.

Holiday accommodation

Most people stayed at a boarding-house when they went away. Bed and breakfast at most seaside resorts cost about 2/6d (12½p) a night in the '30s. Some people already had caravans to tow behind their cars, though,

29 Arriving at the chalet, Blackpool Holiday Camp

and as there were still relatively few of them compared with nowadays, there was no difficulty in finding an empty field owned by a friendly farmer.

In 1937 people were offered an entirely new kind of holiday. This was a seaside holiday camp, and it was the idea of a young Canadian, Billy Butlin. For people without a great deal of money these camps had one outstanding advantage. People knew in advance exactly how much their holiday would cost, including their entertainment. The camps were also immensely popular with children, because there was always something new and exciting to do, whatever the weather was like. Although the holiday camps were temporarily closed because they were needed for war purposes, by the outbreak of the Second World War nearly half a million people had already enjoyed a holiday at "Butlin's".

Children's holidays

There were not many holidays specifically for children between the Wars. School outings (when they existed at all) were almost invariably just day trips. Scouts and Guides regularly went away to camp, however. In fact, the first Scout camp (to Brownsea Island, near Poole, in Dorset) was held as early as 1907.

There was also an exciting new development for the fourteen-year-olds and over.

30   Camden Town Girl Guides at camp at Le Touquet, April 1922

This was the establishment in 1930 of the Youth Hostels Association. It was the first really successful attempt to provide a network of overnight shelters for hikers, rock-climbers and any other young people who wanted to spend a holiday in the country.

By 1939 there were nearly 300 of these hostels, mostly in areas regarded as being of outstanding natural beauty or interest. In some cases they were converted farm-houses, village schools or even water-mills. In other cases they had been specially built within easy reach of some particular local attraction. The accommodation was simple, but clean and reasonably comfortable. The young people could either pay for a meal or else cook their own food in a communal kitchen. A night's stay cost 6d (2½p), or 1/- (5p) for people over 18, and everyone had to arrive either on foot or on a bicycle.

Summer holidays very rarely lasted more than one week in the '30s. The reason was that most people were not paid while they were on holiday, and could not afford to stay away longer. Even when holidays with pay became fairly widespread, shortly before the Second World War, hardly anyone was allowed more than one week's holiday with pay every year.

Few of the really poor families ever had the chance of a holiday at all, of course. But there were some exceptions, like some of the very poorest people in the East End of London. Every year in late summer whole coach-loads of happy Cockneys, from grandparents to babies-in-arms, left the city for a few weeks' working holiday in the hop-fields of Kent.

8 Growing Up on the Dole

One of the most famous cartoons between the Wars appeared in *Punch* in 1932. It showed a little girl from one of the "depressed areas" being offered a drink of milk by a nurse in a hospital. "How far down can I drink?" the child is asking. The idea that she might be allowed to have a whole glass of milk for herself was something that clearly never occurred to her.

31 A group of unemployed ex-service men sing to a theatre queue in 1932, hoping they might be given some money

32   London slums, Padstow Place, Limehouse, 1925

This cartoon must have brought many better-off people up with a jolt. Most of them had little or no idea how the children in the depressed areas were living at that time. But for the children of the three million unemployed, and other desperately poor families, to have to share a glass of milk was a part of everyday life between the Wars.

To get some idea of the poverty that existed in Britain at the time it is only necessary to look at the unemployment pay, or "dole", as it was usually called.

In the early 1920s the maximum an unemployed man with a wife and three children could receive was 29/3d (about £1-48p) a week. At the same period the British Medical Association estimated that a family of this

33   Crowded conditions

size needed to spend at least 22/6½d (£1-13p) on food every week to remain in reasonable health. Added to this, the rent of the worst slum tenement was about 6/- (30p) a week, which left practically nothing for fuel and clothing, let alone such luxuries as toys for the children.

Housing

One of the worst aspects of life for these poor families was usually their appalling housing. Hundreds of thousands of people, especially in the poverty-stricken North, had to live in squalid "back-to-back" homes. These were unbelievably ugly, cramped, terraced houses, with no garden at all in the front and only a tiny, communal yard at the back.

Slum clearance went on, but it was pitifully slow. By 1930 there were still 40,000 "back-to-back" houses in Birmingham, and almost as many in Leeds. Many of them had only one tap, situated outside in the yard, to be shared by four or five families, and sometimes only one toilet, also outside in the yard.

The worst horror of these slum houses, though, were the bedbugs. These found their way not only into every piece of bedding in the house, but even into the furniture. Some local authorities blamed the tenants, and said they were dirty, but no amount of cleaning and scrubbing would get rid of the bedbugs once they had penetrated into the cracks in the walls. The great majority of slum-dwellers also suffered from head-lice. These were passed from person to person, and in the overcrowded slums they were extremely hard to eradicate. The result was that many children could not sleep properly at night because of the bugs and the lice, and woke up in the morning feeling exhausted and fretful.

Some of the luckier slum-dwellers were re-housed in new blocks of flats. These first appeared in most of the large cities in the early 1920s. The standard of the flats varied considerably, however, and within a few

years some had deteriorated so much that they were little better than the slum properties they had replaced. As late as 1927, for instance, many council flats in London had only a share of a bathroom. (Some councillors argued that the poor were so ignorant that they would only keep coal in the baths, anyway.) On the other hand, some flats had such modern amenities as clothes-drying spaces, pram sheds, separate balconies for each flat, club-rooms and play areas for the children.

Food

Another grave problem between the Wars was that poor children were often inadequately fed. Many of them lived mainly on bread and margarine, which was cheap but contained very little nourishment. One result of this malnutrition was that countless children developed rickets (a kind of bone disease), and thousands of them became deformed or even died every year.

The government was well aware of the situation. Indeed, as early as 1921 an act was passed to provide free school dinners for any children who were not progressing at school "by reason of lack of food". But it is difficult to prove that a child is suffering from malnutrition, and as late as 1939 only approximately 4% of the nation's children were receiving free meals. In some cases the children actually refused the meals. For one thing, they sometimes felt that there was a stigma attached to having to go to the special "dinner centres". For another, the food was often far from appetizing. At best, it was some kind of soup or stew, but at other times it was merely potatoes, gravy and bread.

Illness

Not surprisingly, the slum children were constantly ill. Measles, diphtheria and scarlet fever alone killed many thousands of poor children every year. The most dreaded disease was tuberculosis, though, which was often

directly attributable to the children's poor living conditions and their inadequate diet.

When children were seriously ill they were naturally taken to hospital. But there were often no special children's wards, and even toddlers had to share the wards with the adults. It was also the policy in many hospitals not to allow parents to visit their

34   A café in Lambeth Walk

sick children, and it must have been an extremely disturbing experience for many children not only to be ill but also to be deserted, as they thought, by the people they knew and loved best.

Many families tried desperately to make

47

some extra money. Sometimes the mothers were lucky enough to find a job as a "char", which meant scrubbing and cleaning for some better-off family. In most cases, though, all the people in the depressed areas were equally poor, and there was no one with sufficient money to be able to pay for a "char". Other families turned in desperation to the pawnbroker. At first they would pawn such little luxuries as a watch, a clock or a wedding-ring. But as time went on they were often forced to pawn their blankets or even their tables and chairs, and life became more and more squalid and hopeless.

9 Child Welfare

Falling birth-rate
This was a cause of great concern between the Wars. In fact, some people predicted that the population of the country would soon be almost as small as it had been in the Middle Ages. Even worse, a large number of children died in infancy every year, usually through lack of any adequate antenatal or post-natal care. As late as 1931 nearly seven children in a hundred died before they had had their first birthday. This proportion varied considerably from one area of the country to another, however. In some parts of the poverty-stricken North nearly twelve babies in a hundred died in infancy, while in some prosperous parts of the South the figure was as low as four in a hundred.

Birth
Many of the better-off mothers gave birth to their babies in comfortable nursing-homes. They usually stayed there for at least a fortnight, and could be attended by their own doctor if they wished. Other well-off mothers had their children at home, but they engaged a qualified maternity nurse to live in, usually for several weeks both before and after the baby's birth.

Most ordinary working-class women also had their babies at home. But they received little of the skilful care and attention that was given to the mothers who were able to pay. There was often no clinic within reach where they could go for help or advice, and most of them were far too poor to be able to afford to consult a doctor. The only assistance most of them received was from an un-trained midwife. The average charge for this was 30/- (£1.50p), but many midwives were quite willing to accept a few shillings. For many of them delivering babies was only a part-time occupation, in any case, which they did in conjunction with some totally different sort of job, such as running a shop.

Pre-school-age children
There were no play-groups of any kind between the Wars. And although local authorities were allowed to provide nursery schools from 1922 onwards, very few of them did so. This meant that "only children" (without any brothers or sisters), who were extremely common at that time, often had no other children to play with until they were old enough to go to school.

At school
Between the Wars beginning school often meant catching some infectious illness. All the childish infectious diseases were rife in the crowded classrooms, and without modern drugs were often extremely serious. There was nothing parents could do to protect their children, however, as there was no immunization against any of the infectious diseases, with the exception of smallpox. Every year between three and four thousand people (mainly children) died from diphtheria. Another two thousand (almost entirely children) died every year from whooping-cough. Measles and scarlet fever were also dreaded, because even in cases where they were not fatal they often left life-

35 A medical examination at Highbury County School, 1937

long after-effects, such as deafness or poor sight.

There were medical inspections in schools as early as 1907. In fact, all children had to have a medical examination when they entered the elementary school and again when they left. It was not until 1918, however, that the local authorities had a duty to see that children received treatment, and even then no action was usually taken unless a child was seriously ill. It was in 1907 that local authorities first had the right to supply children with glasses. And it was in the same year that they first had the right to set up school dental clinics. Even between the Wars it was still difficult to persuade parents to co-operate with the school dental service, however, as most of them had never brushed their own teeth, and could not understand why their children should be expected to do so.

36 A dental inspection at Mount Pleasant Lane School, London, 1937

37 Children, all in spectacles, at St Anne's School, Brookfield, London, c. 1925

Children at work

In 1918 the compulsory school-leaving age was raised from 12 to 14. But children of 12 and over were still allowed to spend only half the day at school and the other half at work. Not many children could actually find half-day employment, however, except in some parts of the North, and in 1922 "half-timing" was abolished for good. Children of 12 and over were still allowed to work for two hours a day, however, providing it was

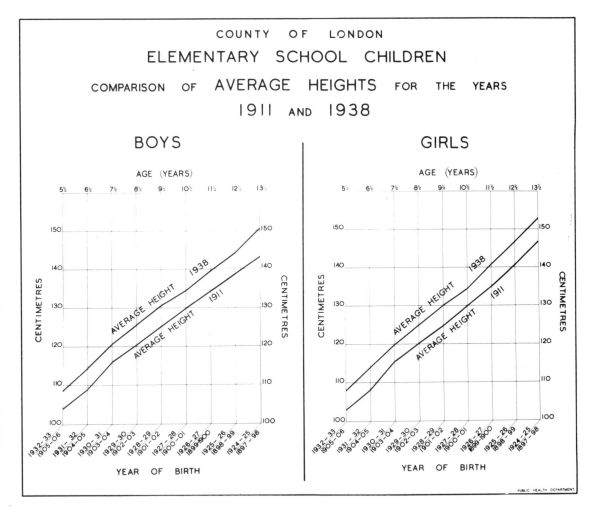

COUNTY OF LONDON
ELEMENTARY SCHOOL CHILDREN
COMPARISON OF AVERAGE HEIGHTS FOR THE YEARS
1911 AND 1938

BOYS   GIRLS

38 A graph, published by the Public Health Department showing increase in children's average height from 1911 to 1938

only for one hour in the morning before school and for one hour afterwards. This meant that newsagents could still employ children to deliver papers, for instance. But no child of school age was permitted to work for even the shortest period in a mine or a factory.

Children and the Law
As early as 1908 there had been special courts for children who broke the law. But except for the fact that they dealt only with child offenders, they differed very little from any other courts. In 1932, however, a new act was passed which said that juvenile courts must "have regard to the welfare of the child or young person". In other words, the aim must be to educate rather than to punish.

The age at which a child could be considered guilty of an offence was also raised from 7 to 8 years old. (This was considerably below the age in any other European country.) In addition, in the case of a child between 8 and 14, the court had to be satisfied that the child knew that what he had done was wrong before any action could be taken. The act also laid down that there must be special magistrates for juvenile courts, appointed from people who had had previous experience of dealing with children and young people. Moreover, the court had to look into the home background of every child, and if necessary arrange for the child to be placed in the care of foster-parents, or in a suitable hostel.

Family difficulties

There were very few broken homes between the Wars. Divorces were not easy to obtain, and were far too expensive for most ordinary working-class people. It was also extremely difficult for a married woman to find any kind of employment, except as a charwoman, and so most women were forced to stay with their husbands on economic grounds. This meant that many children were brought up in extremely unhappy homes, with parents who would much rather have gone their own separate ways. In addition, a great deal of unhappiness was caused by parents who were constantly drunk, as drunkenness was a major problem between the Wars in all levels of society.

10 Town and Country

On the roads

Even between the Wars the roads were dangerous places. In fact, as many children were killed in 1933 as today, although there were only one-sixth as many cars. The reason was partly that children were not taught road safety, and partly that people were not yet fully accustomed to all the cars, lorries and buses that were replacing most of the old horse-drawn vehicles.

39   The car was on its way to the Motor Show at Olympia, 1929. The tricyclist was probably a regular user of the road. The dangers of the road were possibly not fully recognized between the Wars

40 A milkman in Brighton, January 1938. His milk "pram" was a self-propelled vehicle and had to carry an "L" plate until the dairyman had passed his test of "competence to drive"

By the late 1930s it was, in general, only the door-to-door tradesmen, like the milk-man, the coalman and the laundry-man, who were still making use of a horse and cart. But

41 A knife-grinder in Axminster

people like removal men, who had extremely heavy loads, sometimes used a large horse-drawn wagon, although for longer journeys they usually transferred their loads to the railway.

Children were naturally delighted when a horse stopped outside their house. If it was not wearing a nosebag, they would often give it a piece of sugar they had ready. And in poorer areas, in particular, the children would run out with a bucket and shovel, so that they could scoop up any manure for their gardens that the horse might have left on the road!

Street-traders

As well as horse-drawn carts, there were plenty of hand-carts between the Wars. Street-traders, or hawkers, used to push them from street to street, shouting out what they had to sell as they went. Most of the hawkers sold such things as fruit, vegetables and fish, which the housewife had to buy fresh whenever she needed them in the days before deep freezers and fridges. For most children the favourite street-hawker was the rag-and-bone man, though. Everyone knew when he was coming even before they saw him, because of his cry, "Any old rags! Any old iron!". Then he would give the children a few pennies for almost any old rubbish they gave him, and if they had collected some jam-jars he would usually give them a goldfish in exchange!

The first mobile ice-cream man appeared between the Wars (picture 1). He pedalled a tricycle with a large cold-box on the front, labelled "Stop me and Buy one". He sold the first factory-made ice-creams and ice-lollies, because before this time there had only been street-sellers (usually Italian) selling home-made ice-cream in cones.

Door-to-door traders

All kinds of people went from door to door between the Wars. One of them was the knife-grinder, who had a kind of home-made machine that was made out of an old bicycle.

He sat on the saddle and pedalled, and this turned a small grindstone, against which he could sharpen people's scissors and knives, and, in the summer, their garden shears. Tinkers also went round, although not so much in the more prosperous '30s. They had little metal patches which they used for repairing holes in saucepans and kettles. There were also gipsies selling pegs and "lucky heather", who would threaten to put a curse on any housewife who did not buy anything or give them any money.

In addition, there were vast numbers of door-to-door salesmen. These were mainly ex-servicemen, who had fought in the War but had not been able to find a regular job afterwards. They usually sold rather poor quality goods at high prices, but many kindly housewives, rather than turn them completely away, would buy some small article out of pity.

Travel

Most children between the Wars went to the nearest elementary school, and so it was generally only the children attending secondary schools who had to travel by public transport every day. On the other hand, children used public transport to go to the cinema or to visit friends much more between the Wars than they do today because far fewer families had their own cars.

In the '20s double-decker buses still had no roofs. So, when the conductor cried, "Full up inside!", that was exactly what he meant. Anyone else who got on the bus then had to go up the stairs (which were not covered in any way) and sit on the top deck exposed to the wind and the rain or whatever the weather might be.

42 A tram on Westminster Bridge, 1931

As well as buses, there were trams. These also had their upper decks open to the air, at least until the late '20s. Trams could be driven from either end, and so they did not have to be turned round when they reached their terminus. The passengers' seats also had movable backs, so that the passengers could always sit facing forwards. Trams were not very popular, though, because they were slow and noisy. Some people also thought they were dangerous, because they could not pull into the kerb to pick up and set down passengers. And so, in the '30s trolley-buses began to appear instead. Like the trams, they used electricity from overhead wires, but they did not run on lines.

In the country

In the country, life changed rapidly between the two Wars. Improved methods of transport meant that even the most isolated families could visit a town from time to time. And with the coming of the wireless in the late '20s the country children could listen to exactly the same programmes as the children in the cities.

Farming

Methods of farming changed considerably between the Wars. Most farmers began to give up mixed farming and to concentrate on livestock, with just enough arable farming to supply their own fodder. There were even "battery hens" for intensive egg production from the early '20s onwards, so that the old-fashioned farmyard with its scratching poultry became less and less common.

Farm machinery was naturally becoming much more mechanized. Well before the First World War there had been tractors suitable for ploughing and for providing power for such heavy jobs as threshing. Then in 1925 the first light tractor was put on the market. It could cope with mowing and raking, and any other everyday task that called for

59

mobility. Some farmers were even using air-craft for spraying their crops as early as 1930, while others were experimenting with aircraft for sowing some of their seeds. Nevertheless, there were still nearly three-quarters of a million horses in regular work on farms as late as 1939, and most country children between the Wars must have been for many rides on their backs.

43 *Right* Three horses drawing the cutter through the corn in the Chiltern Hills, near Amersham

44 Carey Ostler, aged 15, who had won the first scholarship in farriery awarded by the Dorset Agricultural Committee. The committee's aim was to encourage young men to follow country crafts, which were thought to be dying. Carey's apprentice-ship lasted 3 years, and he earned 10s a week

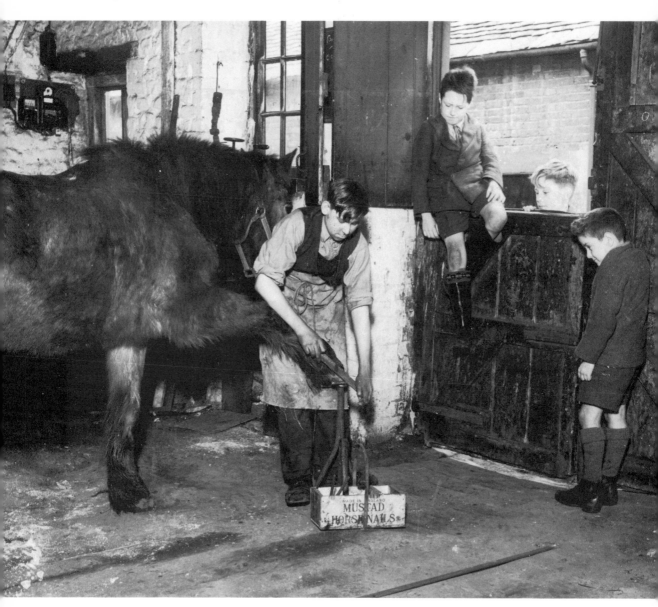

Faces in the News

45   Lady Astor

47   Andrew Bonar Law

46   David Lloyd George

48   Stanley Baldwin

49   James Ramsay Macdonald

52   King George VI

50   Margaret Grace Bondfield

53   Arthur Neville Chamberlain

51   King George V

Table of Major Events in Britain and Abroad

	BRITAIN	ABROAD
1919	The Housing Act gave local authorities the task of building new homes. *Lady Astor* became the first woman M.P. Violence flared up in Ireland.	The Peace Conference ended with the signing of the Treaty of Versailles. Alcock and Brown flew the Atlantic.
1920	Dame Nellie Melba made one of the earliest radio broadcasts, from Chelmsford, Essex.	The League of Nations was set up.
1921	The miners went on strike. The first Northern Ireland Parliament met in Belfast. The Irish Free State was founded.	Violent disorders continued in India.
1922	*Lloyd George* resigned, and *Bonar Law* became Prime Minister. Civil War broke out in Ireland.	Benito Mussolini became Prime Minister of Italy.
1923	*Stanley Baldwin* became Prime Minister. The first Cup Final was held at Wembley.	The Ruhr area of Germany was occupied by the French. Adolf Hitler's Munich Rising failed.
1924	The first Labour Government was formed, with *Ramsay Macdonald* as Prime Minister.	Britain recognized the USSR, and the two countries signed a commercial treaty.
1925	Britain returned to the gold standard. The seamen went on strike in protest against wage cuts.	The Locarno Pact was signed.
1926	The General Strike lasted from May 4th-12th. The National Grid system began to transmit electricity. The first traffic lights were installed in the streets.	
1927	The new Prayer Book was rejected by Parliament.	Britain broke off diplomatic relations with the USSR. An American, Charles Lindbergh, made the first solo flight across the Atlantic, from New York to Paris.

1928	The age at which women could vote was lowered from 30 to 21. The first popular "talkie" was screened, called "The Singing Fool", with Al Jolson. John Logie Baird transmitted television pictures from London to New York.	
1929	*Margaret Bondfield* became the first woman Cabinet Minister. Alexander Fleming discovered penicillin.	The Wall Street Crash in America affected world economy.
1930	Unemployment rose to 2½ million. Oswald Mosley formed a Fascist party. The airship R.101 crashed. Amy Johnson flew solo from England to Australia.	The Allied occupation of Germany ended.
1931	Ramsay Macdonald formed the National Government. The dole was made subject to a Means Test. Britain was forced off the gold standard.	Japanese troops invaded Manchuria (China).
1932	The unemployed staged a Hunger March on London. Britain abandoned Free Trade, and made special agreements with countries within the Empire.	F.D. Roosevelt was elected President of America. Eamon de Valera became President of the Irish Free State.
1933	Unemployment reached nearly 3 million.	Hitler became the German Chancellor. Germany and Japan withdrew from the League of Nations. A truce was signed between Japan and China, leaving the Japanese in occupation of northern China.
1934	The liner "Queen Mary" was launched.	Mao-tse Tung led the Chinese Communists on the Long March.
1935	Baldwin became Prime Minister of a National Government. Watson-Watt developed radar.	Mussolini invaded Abyssinia (now Ethiopia). The Nuremberg Laws outlawed the Jews in Germany. Chiang Kai-shek was elected President of the Chinese Executive.
1936	*King George V* died and was succeeded by his son, Edward VIII. A few months later the new king abdicated and was succeeded by his brother, *George VI*. The Jarrow Crusade marched on	Civil War broke out in Spain.

London.
The BBC began the first television transmissions from Alexandra Palace.

1937   *Neville Chamberlain* became Prime Minister, and adopted a policy of appeasement towards Hitler and Mussolini.
The first jet engine was developed.

Fighting continued in Spain.
Fighting was renewed between Japan and China.

1938   Threats of war caused Chamberlain to go to Munich to meet Hitler.
Preparations were made for war.
The liner "Queen Elizabeth" was launched.
Nylon was first produced.

Hitler annexed Austria, and claimed the Sudetenland from Czechoslovakia.

1939   Britain promised to support Poland if attacked by Germany.
On September 3rd war was declared on Germany.

Hitler broke the Munich agreement, and occupied the whole of Czechoslovakia.
Italy seized Albania.
On September 1st German troops marched into Poland.

Glossary

artificial silk   a lustrous fabric used as a silk substitute, made not from the thread of silkworms but from cellulose or some similar substance

bakelite   a hard, strong, synthetic resin, which can be moulded and used in the manufacture of many articles as a substitute for wood

bedbug   a brown, wingless insect which sucks blood from human beings at night

bob   a woman's hairstyle when hair is cut short and square across the forehead

charabanc   a long, open coach with transverse seats, used for excursions, tours etc

charwoman   a woman hired by the hour to do odd jobs of domestic work, especially scrubbing

copper   a large vessel for boiling clothes

depression   a slump in trade

dole   a weekly payment to unemployed workmen under the National Insurance Act

electric organ   an organ on which the sound is produced by electrical devices

fender   a kerb in front of a fire to prevent live coal or ashes falling beyond the hearth

gaiter   a covering of cloth or leather fitting over the upper part of a shoe, and over the ankle and up to or over the knee

gramophone   an instrument for reproducing sounds, such as speech and music, by means of a revolving disc; a record-player

hike   a planned walking-tour, especially carrying one's luggage in a pack or a rucksack

jerry-built   built of shoddy material; in the case of houses, built of flimsy, second-rate materials, cheaply and hastily, by a speculative builder

linoleum   a kind of durable floor-covering, made of coarse hessian on the underside, and on the upperside of a mixture of linseed oil, cork, gum, etc

mangle   a roller with a handle at one end, for extracting the water from wet clothes and other kinds of linen, and for smoothing them

marcel wave   a temporary, artificial wave put into straight hair by means of hot curling tongs

panama	a hat made of fine, pliant, straw-like material
parquet	a flooring made of wooden blocks, instead of boards
plus-fours	wide, baggy knickerbockers, worn by golfers
radiogram	a combination of a radio and a gramophone
rayon	a synthetic fibrous material, made from cellulose to resemble silk
ribbon development	the tendency to build continuously along main roads, without corresponding development in the areas lying behind the roads
rickets	a disease of children, characterized by softness and curvature of the bones, which usually results in bow-legs or knock-knees, due to a faulty diet lacking in vitamin D
scooter	a child's toy, consisting of a flat board mounted on two wheels, on which one foot rests, which is propelled by the other foot, and guided by a tall steering handle attached to the front wheel
shingle	a style of hairdressing for women, in which the hair is cropped close to the nape of the neck
tango	a South American dance in two-four time
tinker	a mender of pots, kettles, etc, especially one who travels round the countryside
trolley-bus	a bus driven by electric power supplied by an overhead conductor, but not running, like a tram, on rails

Places to Visit

Abbot Hall Museum of Lakeland Life and Industry, Kendal, Cumbria
Abbots Hall Museum of Rural Life in East Anglia, Stowmarket, Suffolk
Abergavenny and District Museum, Castle House, Abergavenny
Ashwell Village Museum, Swan Street, Ashwell, Herts
Beaulieu Abbey National Motor Museum, Beaulieu, Hants
Belfast Transport Museum, Witham Street, Belfast
Birmingham Museum of Science and Industry, Newhall Street, Birmingham
Bowes Museum, Barnard Castle, Co. Durham
Cambridge and County Folk Museum, Castle Street, Cambridge
Castle Museum, Norwich
Castle Museum, York
Glasgow Transport Museum, Albert Drive, Glasgow
Gloucester Folk Museum, Westgate Street, Gloucester
Kirkstall Abbey Museum, near Leeds
Letchworth Museum, Herts
Museum of Domestic Life, South Quay, Great Yarmouth, Norfolk
Museum of English Rural Life, The University, Reading, Berks
Museum of London, London Wall, London
North of England Open Air Museum, Beamish Hall, Beamish, Co. Durham
Pollocks Toy Museum, Scala Street, London, W.1
Provost Skene's House, Guest Row, Aberdeen
Railway Museum, Queen Street, York
Shuttleworth Collection of Historic Aeroplanes and Cars, Old Warden Aerodrome, Beds
Ulster Folk Museum, Cultra Manor, Holywood, Belfast
Victoria and Albert Museum, London

Books for Further Reading

Non-fiction

Britain in the Twentieth Century by R.J. Unstead (A. & C. Black Ltd)

A History of Everyday Things in England Volume V (1914-1968) by S.E. Ellacott (B.T. Batsford Ltd, 1968)

How We Used to Live by Freda Kelsall (Macdonald Educational Ltd)

Later than We Thought by René Cutforth (David and Charles Ltd)

Leslie Baily's BBC Scrapbook Volume 2 (1918-1939) by Leslie Baily (Allen and Unwin Ltd)

Life in Britain between the Wars by L.C.B. Seaman (B.T. Batsford Ltd, 1970)

This is Your Century by Geoffrey Trease (Heinemann)

The Twentieth Century by Peter Lane (B.T. Batsford Ltd, 1972)

Fiction

The Family from One End Street by Eve Garnett (Frederick Muller Ltd) (and other books in the same series)

The Oak and the Ash by Frederick Grice (Oxford University Press)

Swallows and Amazons by Arthur Ransome (Jonathan Cape Ltd) (and other books by the same author)

Index